A TO Z : ULTIMATE GUIDE AND HACKING WITH KALI LINUX

*Best complied knowledge on Practical
Guide to Computer Network Hacking,
Encryption,Cybersecurity, Penetration Testing
for Beginners. The Secrets of VPN Services,
Firewalls and the Linux Command Line*

ISBN: 9798695970241

Imprint: Independently published

◆ ◆ ◆

INTRODUCTION

I am very much delighted to see that you all have shown so much interest in learning about the basics and usefulness of Kali Linux. Kali Linux is one of the most effective software of today. It can also be regarded as a boon for all computing and networking people.

Kali Linux does the job of a security auditing software and it also helps in various aspects of networking and hacking. Kali Linux comes along with various information and security-related tasks such as reverse engineering, penetration testing and security research. Computer forensics.

is also a part of Kali Linux. Each and every service which is provided by Kali Linux is certified and comes along with all-over control along with wider aspects of accreditations.

Kali Linux belongs to the family of Linux distribution. Cyber security is the prime concern of this Linux distribution. Many of the companies today take help of Kali Linux for checking and tracing out their vulnerabilities for ensuring 100% security of their infrastructure. It is an opensource program and is thus totally free. Not only that but it is completely legal and can be used for various scenarios in an enterprise or organization.

CHAPTER 1: BASICS OF HACKING

Hacking is nothing but unauthorized intrusion within a network or computer which is executed by attackers known as hackers . The attackers try to attack those
systems which are vulnerable to threats. They keep their prying eyes open all the time, searching around for vulnerabilities. They can act as an individual or even work in a group. Not only might that but the hackers also function as a part of an organization which works with the motive of disrupting the functionalities of other organizations. Most of the time they try to alter the system of an organization and target the security   infrastructure for breaching of information and
gaining access. However, hackers not only work as attackers but also use their skills for finding out the

weak spots along with the various vulnerabilities within a system. This is also carried out for finding and mending the weaknesses for preventing all forms of malicious attacks from entering the system.

Different Types Of Hackers

There are various types of hackers in the world of hacking which perform different types of functions. The types of hackers help in defining the relationship
between the systems and hackers which are trying to attack. The most common types of hackers are:

Black Hat Hackers: The term black hat had its origin from the old Western movies in which the villains used to wear black hats. The black hat hackers act as
individuals who try to have unauthorized access into the system of an organization or network for the
purpose of exploiting the security infrastructure for various malicious reasons. The hackers of this type do not come with any sort of authority or permission for
compromising the targets. They attempt to do damage by compromising the infrastructure of the security systems, shutting down the systems or also by altering the primary functions of a website or network. The primary intention of the black hat hackers is to gain all-over access or steal the information regarding finances, access various passwords or gain insights into other forms of personal data.

White Hat Hackers: The white hat hackers are the second type of hackers but they act as the good guys. The white hat hackers work with various organizations for the purpose of strengthening the security of any system. The white hat hackers come with all sorts of permissions for engaging the targets and also compromise the

same within the provided boundary of rules. The white hat hackers are also known as ethical hackers. The ethical hackers specialize in this field with various forms of ethical tools and techniques meant for hacking. They use special methodologies for securing up the
information system of an organization. Contrary to the black hat hackers, the ethical hackers exploit the security system of a network and then check out for the backdoors after being legally permitted to perform so. The ethical hackers always point out all forms of vulnerabilities that they dig out from the systems of the organizations to make sure that the gaps are mended for preventing exploitation by the malicious attackers.

Grey Hat Hackers: The grey hat hackers gain access to the security systems of the organizations and networks in the same way just like black hat hackers do. But the grey hat hackers perform such actions without any form of malicious intent and disclose the vulnerabilities along with the loopholes to the agencies of law enforcement or various intelligence agencies. The grey hat hackers generally surf the internet and hack the
computer systems for notifying the owners or the administrator of the network or system which contains various vulnerabilities which need to be mended immediately. The grey hat hackers might also extort the hacked systems by offering to inform about the defects for some fees too.

Common Tools Of Hacking

For accomplishing the act of hacking, the hackers implement various types of techniques. Let's have a look at some of them.

Rootkits: Rootkit acts like a program or a huge set of software which allows the attackers to gain complete access or control of a

system or network which directly
connects or interacts with the system of the internet. Rootkit was first introduced as a system of backdoor process for fixing various issues in regards to software. However,today this software is widely being used by the hackers for disrupting the functionality and control of a system from its actual owner or administrators. There are various ways in which rootkits can be installed in the system of the victim. The most common way of installing rootkit is by implementing phishing attacks along with social engineering.Once the rootkits have been installed in the system of the victim,
the attacker gains access to the system secretly and controls the overall functioning with which they can
easily steal confidential data and information and can also shut down a system
completely.

Keyloggers: This is a very special type of tool which has been designed for recording and logging each and every key pressed on the victim system. The keyloggers record the stroke of the keys by staying attached to the Application Programming Interface or API. It tracks the key strokes when anything is being typed by using the keyboard in a system. The files which are recorded are then saved which contains various forms of information such as details regarding website visit, usernames, the record of opened applications, screenshots, bank details and many more. The keyloggers are also capable
of capturing the personal messages, credit card details, passwords, mobile numbers and various other details which are generally typed in a system. The keyloggers generally arrive as a malware which allows the cybercriminals to breach all forms of sensitive data.

Vulnerability scanner: A vulnerability scanner is used for the purpose of classifying and then detecting various forms of weaknesses in a system, network, communication system, computers etc. This is one of the most common forms of tool which is being used by the ethical hackers for finding out the potential vulnerabilities and loopholes and then fixes them up on urgent basis. However, a vulnerability scanner can also be used by the black hat hackers for checking the vulnerabilities and weak spots within a system and then finding out the proper tool for exploiting the same.

Techniques Of Hacking

There are various techniques which are being used by the hackers for exploiting a system.

SQL Injection: SQL or structured query language has been designed for the purpose of exploiting various forms of data in the database of the victim. This form of attack falls under the cyber attack which targets the databases via the statements of SQL for tricking the systems. This form of attack is generally carried out by the use of website interface which attempts in issuing the commands of SQL through a database for hacking the passwords, usernames and other related information related to the database. All those websites along with web applications which are coded poorly are very much prone to the SQL injection attacks. This is because the applications which are based on the web contains various user input fields like login pages, search pages, request forms related to support and products, comments section and many others which are very
much susceptible to the attacks and can be very easily hacked by simple manipulation of the codes.

DDoS or Distributed Denial of Service: It is a form of hacking attack in which the normal traffic of a server is distorted from entering the server and floods the traffic of the network. This ultimately results in denial of service as it serves just like a traffic jam which clogs the roads and also prevents the regular form of traffic from reaching the destination. All the devices of today such as IoT devices, computers, mobile phones etc. which connects with the network are very much prone to the attacks of DDoS.

MAC Spoofing: Each and every form of device which are used by the people today come with network interface controller or NIC. It helps the users to connect with the network such as with the internet directly. The NIC of each device is accompanied with a MAC address which is assigned after various processes of hard coding. The MAC spoofing attack is a very deadly form of attack in which the hackers hide themselves and their system behind a customized and false MAC address. This reduces the risks on the part of the hackers from getting caught. So, you might give access to a new

system thinking of it to be absolutely legitimate but it might happen that a hacker will hide himself behind a false MAC address which you cannot even realize. By using this technique, the hackers can easily hack internet connection via Wi-Fi and can also gain access to all those devices which are connected to each other via LAN. The technique of MAC spoofing also leads to several forms of other serious crimes in which the hackers steal the identity of someone else and carries on with some serious form of data breaching in which someone will be held as guilty without even knowing about the actual hacker. However, there are various OS in the market today such as MAC and Windows which can easily connect with the LAN without using the MAC address.

CHAPTER 2: WHAT IS ETHICAL HACKING?

Ethical hacking is also called as intrusion testing, penetration testing and also red teaming. In simple words, it is the controversial technique of finding out vulnerabilities and weaknesses in a system simply by imitating the actions and intent of the malicious hackers. An ethical hacker is a person or security professional who uses his skills for the purpose of various defensive measures on part of the administrators of an information system.

An ethical hacker is also known as a white hat or white hat hacker. By conducting various tests, an ethical hacker tries to find out the answers to the following questions : What are the

locations, systems or information can the attacker gain access?
What will the attacker see before setting his target?
What will the attacker do with the information which is available in the system?
Is anyone able to notice the various attempts made by the attacker to gain access?
The ethical hacker who has been given the job of
penetration testing operates on the permission
along with the knowledge of that organization for which he has been assigned the job of defense.
There are various cases in which an organization will not be informing the security information team about all the activities which is going to be carried out by the ethical hacker just for testing the effectiveness and concise of the security information team. This whole thing is also known as double blind environment. For the purpose of effective and legal operation, the
organization needs to inform an ethical hacker about all those assets and information which are meant to be
protected, the potential sources of threats and the limit to which the organization will be supporting the efforts of the ethical hacker.

Process Of Ethical Hacking

All the ethical hackers follow a strict process in order to get the best usable and to the point legal results. Let's have a look at the processes which are followed by the ethical hackers.

Planning

No matter what kind of project it is, for every successful project planning is of utmost importance. It provides the ethical hackers with the opportunity of thinking about what are the things that need to be done, set the goals which are to be reached and also for the assessments of risks for evaluating how to carry out a complete project. There are various factors which are

considered by the ethical hackers before carrying out a project of ethical hacking. The list of factors includes culture, policies of security, laws, regulations, requirements of the industry and best practices. All of these factors play an important role in the process of decision making when it comes to the initiation of ethical hacking.The phase of planning in ethical hacking will be having an overall influence on how the process

of hacking is being performed, the information which is collected and shared and will also be directly influencing the integration and delivery of the results into the program of security. The planning phase is the very first step and will be describing most of the details about the controlled attack of hacking. It will also be answering all forms of questions regarding hacking

such as how the process of ethical hacking is going to be controlled and supported, what are the basic actions which needs to be performed and for how long will the process go on.

Reconnaissance

It is the process of searching for all those information which are freely available for assisting in the process of attack. This whole process can be as easy and simple as just using a ping or browsing the various newsgroups which are available on the internet for searching that

information which is leaked by the employees or as tough and messy as digging through a huge trash of letter or receipts. This process can also include several other processes such as phone tapping, social engineering, network tapping and also data theft. The process of information searching will be limited only to the extent to which the organization and the ethical hacker will

want to go for the purpose of recovering all the

required information which they are looking out for.

The phase of reconnaissance introduces the deep relationship in between the tasks which needs to be completed and all those methods which will be needed for protecting the information and assets of the organization.

Enumeration

It is also known as vulnerability or network discovery. Enumeration is the process of obtaining all those information which is available readily from the system of the target, networks and application which are used by the target. It is also to be noted that the phase of enumeration is the actual point where the thin line between malicious attacks and ethical hacking gets blurred very often as it is very easy and simple to go outside the dedicated boundaries which have been
outlined in the original plan of attack. For the purpose of creating a clear picture of the environment of an organization, various techniques and tools are being used which are readily available. These available tools include NMap and port scanning. However, it is very easy to collect all the required information, it is very difficult to make sure of the value of information which is available in the hands of the hacker. At the very first glance, the process of enumeration seems to be very simple in which data is collected then evaluated collectively for establishing a proper plan for more searching or
building up a detailed matrix for the analysis or vulnerability phase. However, this phase is the actual phase in which the ability of ethical hacker in taking logical
decisions plays a very important role.

Analysis of vulnerability

For the purpose of effectively analyzing all the data, an ethical hacker needs to employ a pragmatic approach which is logical in nature as well. In the phase of vulnerability analysis, all the information which has been collected is compared with all the known forms of vulnerabilities in the practical process. Any form of in-

formation is useful in the process, no matter from where
it originates or what the source is. A small pinch of information
can also help in finding out some
new sort of vulnerability in the system and might also lead to
several other discoveries of vulnerabilities which have not been
found yet. The known form of vulnerabilities, service packs, incidents, updates along with various hacker tools helps in properly
identifying the point of attack. The internet provides the ethical
hackers with a huge amount of information which can be associated very easily with the system architecture along with weak
and strong points in a system.

Exploitation

A considerable amount of time is spent for the purpose of evaluating and planning an ethical hack. It is very obvious that all of
these planning will lead to some sort of attack. The level of exploitation of a system can be as simple as running a very small
tool in the system or as tough as a collection of many complex
steps which needs to be executed in a proper way for gaining
access to the system. The process of exploitation can be broken
into a collection of subtasks which can be either one single step
or a collection of various steps. As each and every step is performed, a process of evaluation takes place which ensures that
the outcome which has been expected is met. Any form of divergence from the plan of attack can be graded into two parts:
Expectation: Are the expected results of exploitation met or the
results are conflicting with the assumptions of the organization?
Technical: Is the target system behaving in a manner which is not
at all expected, which is actually having an impact on the system
exploitation and the system
engagement in total?

Final analysis

Although the phase of exploitation comes with a huge number of

validations and checks for ensuring the success of the hack, one last final analysis is needed for categorizing the system vulnerabilities in accordance to the exposure level and also for assisting in the drawing up of a plan for mitigation. The phase of final analysis links up the exploitation phase and the deliverable creation. A comprehensive image of the complete attack is needed for the construction of a bigger size picture of the current posture of the security environment of an
organization and also for expressing the vulnerabilities clearly.

Deliverables

Deliverable communicates with the test results in a variety of ways. Some of the deliverables are concise and short in nature which only provides the vulnerabilities list along with the ways in which it can be mended whereas, the other form of deliverables can be detailed and long which will provide a list of the probable vulnerabilities in a system which comes with the description regarding how the vulnerabilities were found, how they can be exploited, the results of having such vulnerabilities within the system and how to fix
the situation. This phase is actually used by an ethical hacker in conveying his hack results to the
organization. It can also be the case if the deliverables do not actually frighten the administrators, the test is considered as a fail.

CHAPTER 3: CYBER SECURITY

In this world of today where technological innovations are taking place every day, the potential threats of cyber attacks are also increasing in equal pace. Cyber security plays a deep role in securing the information and data of the systems and networks in today's world of vulnerability.Cyber security is nothing but the employment of various tools and technologies for the purpose of securing the networks, programs, system data and network from the potential attacks, damages and various forms of unauthorized access. Cyber security is also known as security of information technology.

Cyber Security And Its Importance

Most of the organizations and institutions such as military, government, medical along with financial bodies stores up an accountable amount of data on the systems of computers along with databases which can be found online. In most of the cases, the information which is being stored up in the servers and databases are highly sensitive in nature, leakage of which can result in serious troubles for the concerned organization. Unauthorized access to the systems of the organizations along with the database can lead to data breaching along with the exploitation of the security infrastructure of an organization.The organizations which are targeted might lose up all forms of sensitive data along with complete loss of access to the systems. As the volume of cyber attacks is increasing day by day,
the organizations especially those which are concerned with national health and security are required to take some serious steps for safeguarding all forms of sensitive data. Cyber security is the ultimate option which can help an organization in protecting all its data and servers.

Cyber Security & Encryption

Encryption is the process of encoding communication in such a way so that only the authorized parties can encode the message of communication. It is done by using SSL/TLS and PKI protocols. The very reason why is it important so much stems from the process in which the internet was built up by using the protocol of HTTP. Hypertext Transfer Protocol or HTTP is of the same age that of the internet. HTTP is the protocol of communication which allows the servers in the web and the web browsers for communicating and displaying the information in a proper intended way. When a user visits a website, it is not actually the way it looks in the browser. Websites are built up of a bunch of codes which are sent to the web browsers which are then visually arranged by the browser in the way the web designer intended to do. The main problem of HTTP is that it is not at all secure. So, any person who knows the process can easily spy on the connections of HTTP on the internet. In simple words, a third party can easily read along with manipulate a communication over HTTP between the clients and the servers. Encryption is the technique that actually comes into play in taking care of the

communication by serving the websites over the protocol of HTTPS. HTTPS is the secured version of HTTP. All the connections which are built over HTTPS are encrypted in nature. In simple terms, any form of communication over the protocol of HTTPS is highly secure.Encryption prevents spying on communication by the third parties. In case you are related with

online business and you need to take the financial as well as personal details of the customers,make sure that your website is encrypted so that your customers are not at risk at the time of details exchange.

How Does The Process Of Encryption Work?

The process of encryption begins when the web browser reaches one website which comes with

an SSL certificate. The web server and the browser proceeds with what is known as SSL handshake. At the preliminary stages, the web browser verifies that the SSL certificate which is installed in the website is legitimate in nature and has been issued by a trustworthy authority of certification. After the web browser makes sure that the certificate is legitimate in nature, it starts to negotiate with the terms of the encrypted connection with the server. When it comes to encryption, there are mainly two key pairs. The first is the asymmetric key pair which consists of the private and public keys. These keys have no function with the encryption bulk but they are used for authentication. When a web browser tests the authenticity of SSL certificate of a website, it makes sure that the certificate of SSL which is being questioned is actually the owner of the public form of key. It performs this by using up the public key for encrypting a small packet of data. If the web server is able to decrypt the data packet by using the respective private key and then send the packet back, it is proved that the server is the owner of the public key and everything is stated as verified. In case the web server fails to decrypt the data packet, the certificate of the server is taken as "not trusted". The other key pair is the session keys. This form of keys is generated after the authenticity of the SSL certificate has been verified and all the terms regarding encryption have also been negotiated. While a public key can be used only for encrypting and a private key for decrypting, the session keys can be used for both the functions of encryption and decryption. The session keys are smaller in size and also less secure in nature when compared with the asymmetric form of counterparts. However, the session keys are strong enough for performing both the functions.The server and the web browser use the session keys for the rest of the communication. After leaving the site, the session keys which are being used are discarded and brand-new session keys are generated for the new visit.

Common Types Of Cyber Attacks

Cyber attacks are increasing day by day with the innovations in the world of technology. There are various types of cyber attacks that can be found today where some are used most commonly such as phishing, malware, XSS and many more. Let's have a look at some of the most common types of cyber attacks.

Malware

Malware is a form of harmful software which is used for gaining access to the systems of the victims. The malware can also be called as viruses. Once a malware enters the victim system, it can lead to havoc starting from gaining overall control of the system to the monitoring of all sorts of actions, stealing sensitive data silently and also can lead to a complete shutdown of the
system. The attackers use various ways for inserting malware in the target system. But there are also various cases in which the system users are being tricked into installing a malware in the system.

Phishing

Receiving emails with various unwanted links and
attachments is a very common thing today. Such action of sending out harmful links and attachments via email is known as phishing. In phishing attacks, the attackers send out emails to the targets which seem like a trustable email. Most of the emails come with links and attachments which when clicked leads to the installation
of malware in the system without even the user of the system knowing nothing. Some of the phishing links can also lead the users to a new website which might ask for confidential data such as bank and credit card details. Such websites are actually a trap which is used by the attackers for installing the malware in the target systems.

XSS

Cross-site scripting or XSS attack is used for targeting the users of a website directly. It is somewhat similar to the SQL injection attack and also involves injecting harmful codes in a website. But, in the case of XSS attacks, the websites are not attacked. In an XSS attack, the malicious code which has been injected in the website runs only in the browser of the user and can be used for stealing sensitive data such as username, password, bank details and many more.

Malware And Its Types

Malware is a form of malicious software which is being used for gaining access to the system of the victim. The cyber criminals design malware in a way which can be used for stealing data, compromising the functions of the computer, bypassing the access controls and many more.

Types of malware

There are various types of malware that can be found today. Let's have a look at them.

Adware: Adware are those programs which are used for displaying advertisements on the websites which when clicked redirects to the website which is being advertised and also collects all forms of market data about the user. There are also various forms of pop-up adware that generally contains malicious links which can lead to harm of the system.

Spyware: It is a software which is used for spying the target users. It has been designed for capturing and monitoring the activities of the users on the websites. Adware is also a form of spyware which sends out the activities of browsing of the users to the advertisers.

Worm: Worm is a form of virus which is being used by the cyber-criminals for the purpose of replicating themselves. Worms use computer networks for spreading and can lead to stealing or deletion of data. Many of the worms are also being designed for spreading only through the systems and do not lead to any form of harm to the systems

CHAPTER 4: LINUX ARCHITECTURE

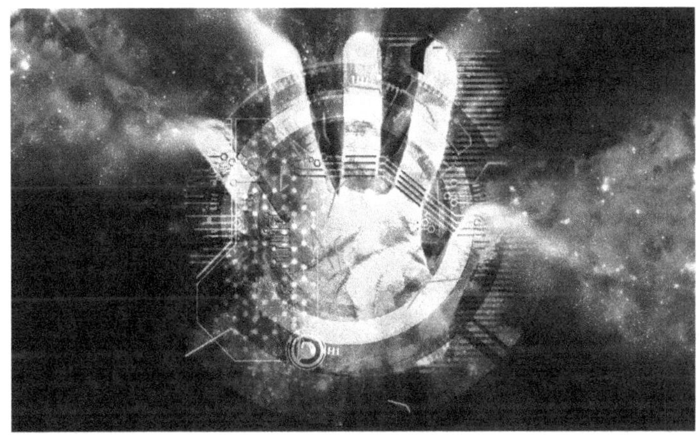

Linux is one of the finest operating systems which can be found today. It is open source in nature and is based on UNIX. It is just a simple OS like the commercial ones like Windows XP, Windows 10 and MAC OS. An OS is nothing but the graphical form of interface between the system of a computer and the user of the system. It comes with the responsibility of managing all the resources related to hardware that the system of a
computer has and also helps in establishing communication in between the hardware and the software.

Open Source Software

An open source software is a software which has its source code available with the license with which the holder of copyright has the right to study the software, change the settings and also distribute the same software with anyone he wants for any form of purpose.

Linux Os And Its Components

The Linux OS is composed of three different components.

The Kernel

The System Library

The System Utility

The Kernel

The kernel functions as the core part of any form of OS. It is responsible for handling the tasks along with the hardware of the system of a computer. The CPU time and memory are the two examples of the entities which are being managed by the kernel. The kernel of an OS is of two types:

Microkernel: The microkernel is a type of OS kernel. As its name goes by, it comes with a very basic form of functionality. It is the least amount of software which can provide with the environment which is required for the functioning of an operating system. This environment of kernel covers management of threads, low level management of address space and inter-process form of communication.

Monolithic kernel: Monolithic kernel is the form of kernel which comes with various drivers along with it. It is an architecture of the operating system in which the operating system of a system works in the space of kernel. This form of the kernel is able to load or unload dynamically all the modules which are executable at the time of running. The monolithic form of kernel stays in the supervisor mode. The major point of difference between the micro kernel and the monolithic kernel is that the monolithic form of kernel can alone define a very high level of interface over the hardware of the system of a computer.

Supervisor mode

The supervisor mode of the monolithic kernel is a flag which mediates from the hardware of a system. It can be easily modified by running the codes in the software system level. All form of system level tasks comes with this flag while they are operating or running. However, the applications of user space do not come with this flag set. The flag makes sure that whether the execution of machine code operations is possible or not such as performing various operations like disabling the interruptions or modifying the registers for various forms of descriptor table. The main idea behind having two different types of operation comes from the idea "with more amount of control come more responsibilities". Any program in the supervisor mode is trusted so much that it will never fail as any form of failure will lead to crashing of the computer system. In simple words, the kernel is the component which is responsible for all form of activities of the OS. It is composed of various types of modules and also directly interacts with the base hardware. The kernel comes with all the necessary abstraction for the purpose of hiding all the low-level details of hardware to system or programs of application.

The System Library

The system library is composed of a collection of resources which are non-volatile in nature and are used up by the resources of the computer system and is mainly used for developing software. This comes with data configuration, help data, documentation, templates for messaging and many more. Generally, the term library is being used for describing a huge collection of implementations regarding behavior which is written down in terms of computer language. It comes with a perfectly defined form of interface which helps in invoking the behavior. So, this means that anyone who wants to create a program of high level can easily use up the system library for the purpose of making system calls continuously. The system library can be requested at a time by various individual forms of programs simultaneously, in order to make sure that the library has been coded in a way so that several programs can use up the library even when the concerned programs are not at all linked nor have a connection with each other. In simple terms, the system libraries are unique programs or form of functions built up of the system utilities or application programs which have access to all the features of the kernel. This form of library implements a majority of the functions related to the
operating system of a computer and they are not required to have the rights of code access for the

module of the kernel.

The System Utility

The programs of system utility are responsible for performing all forms of individual and specialized level tasks. The utility software is a form of system software. It has been designed for running the programs of application and hardware for a system of computer. The system software can also be considered as the interface between the applications of the users and the hardware. In simple words, the system utility software is the software of a system which has been designed for the purpose of configuring, analyzing, optimizing and maintaining a system of computer. The utility software works hand in hand with the operating system for supporting the infrastructure of a system, differentiating it from the software of application which is aimed for performing the various tasks directly which will be benefiting the normal users.

Characteristics Of Linux Architecture

Linux comes with various features that can help the regular users a lot.

Multiuser capability

This is the most unique characteristic of Linux OS in which the resources of a computer such as memory, hard disk etc. can be accessed by various users at a time. However, the users access the resources not from a
single terminal. Each of the users is given an individual terminal for accessing the resources and operating them. A terminal consists of at least one VDU, mouse and keyboard as the devices for input. All the terminals are linked or connected with the primary server or Linux or with the host machine the resources of which

and other peripheral devices like printer can be used by the users.

Multitasking

Linux OS comes with the capability of easily handling various jobs at a time. For example, a user can execute a command for the purpose of execution of a huge list and type in a notepad at the same time. This is intelligently managed by dividing the time of CPU by implementing the policies of scheduling along with the concept of switching of contexts.

Portability

Portability is the feature that made Linux OS so famous among the users. Portability does not mean at all that it can be carried around in CDs, pen drive or memory cars nor the size of the file is small. By portability, it means that the OS of Linux along with all its application can function on various types of hardware in the exact same way. The kernel of Linux and the application programs of the OS support the installation of the same on even those systems which comes with the least configuration of hardware.

Security

Security is considered as the most essential part of any operating system. It is really important for all those users and organizations who are using the system for various forms of confidential tasks. Linux OS comes with various concepts of security for the purpose of protecting the users from any form of unauthorized access of the system and their data.

Main Concepts Of Linux Security

Linux provides 3 main types of security concepts.

Authentication: This helps in authenticating the user with the system by providing login names and password for the individual users so that their work cannot be accessed by any third party.

Authorization: At the file level of Linux OS, it comes with limits of authorization for the users. There are write, read and execution permissions for every file which determines who all can access the files, who can modify the same and who all can execute the files.

Encryption: This feature of Linux OS helps in encoding the user files into a format which is unreadable in
format and is called cyphertext. This makes sure that even if someone becomes successful in opening up the system, the files will be safe.

Communication

Linux OS comes with a great feature for the purpose of communicating with the users. It can be either within the network of one single computer or in between two or more than two networks of a computer. The users of such systems can seamlessly exchange data, mail and programs through the networks.

CHAPTER 5: BASICS OF LINUX OPERATING SYSTEM

Linux is a simple operating system just like other operating systems such as Windows. As an OS,Linux helps in managing the hardware of a system and also provides services that the other software needs for running. It is regarded as a hands-on operating system. For example, if running an OS like Windows is like an automatic car, running Linux OS is like driving a stick. It
might need some more work to do, but once the user gets a nice grip of the functioning of Linux, using the line of commands and also installing the packages will become super easy.

History Of Linux

Linux is similar to the MAC OS X, which is also based on Unix. Unix was developed in the early 1970s with a primary goal of creating an OS which will turn out to be accessible and also secure at the same time for various users. In 1991, Linux was developed with the goal of

distributing the features of Unix. It was launched as open-source software and till date, it is the same. Open source software is a software whose code is visible completely by the user and can also be modified according to need and can be redistributed. Linux is just the kernel and not a complete OS. The kernel provides for an interface between the hardware and requests from the

user applications. The other part of the OS consists of utilities, GNU libraries and various other software. The OS as one complete unit is called as GNU/Linux.

A Bit Of Servers

The Linode that the users have is a type of server. A server is nothing but a type of master computer which helps in providing various forms of service all over the network or across a connected network of computers. The servers are generally:
Stays on all the time.
It is generally connected with the internet or a group of computer networks.
Consists of files and programs for the purpose of website hosting or for other content of the Internet.
As the server acts just like a computer, there are various similarities in between the Linode and the home computer. Some of the similarities are:
The Linode is generally hosted on a physical form of machine. It sits on the available pool of data centers.
Linodes uses up OS like Linux. It is another type of OS similar to Mac or Windows.

Just like a user can easily install various applications in their PC, applications can be installed on Linode as well. All these applications which are installed on a Linode help in performing various tasks like hosting a website.

A user can easily create, edit and delete files just like it can be done on a PC. The user can navigate through the directories as well just like PC. Just like a PC, Linodes are connected with the internet.

Things To Consider Before Installing Linux

Before installing Linux, you need to make sure which distribution of Linux you want to install.Linux OS comes in various versions which are known as distributions. The distributions are similar to that of the
versions of OS like Windows 7 or Windows XP. The new versions of operating systems like Windows are the upgraded versions. But, in case of Linux, the distributions are not upgraded but are of various flavors. Several distributions of Linux install various different software bundles.

Linux Distributions

The major difference between the distributions of Linux tends to be from the aspect of aims and goals of the distribution and which software bundles are installed rather than any form of difference in the Linux kernel code. RedHat Linux which consists of CentOS and Fedora and Debian Linux which consists of Ubuntu shares a huge amount of codes with one another. The
kernels are more or less the same and the applications along with user utilities from the project of
GNU are also similar. Some of the distributions of Linux have been designed to be as minimalistic and simple as possible whereas some has been designed having the current and the best

software of the era. All the distributions of Linux aim at providing the best stability and
reliability to the users. In addition to the individual personality of distributions, you will also need to consider various factors which will help you at the time of choosing your desired distribution.

Release cycle: The various distributions of Linux release the updates of their OS atdifferent schedules. The distributions like Arch Linux and Gentoo uses a model of rolling release in which each individual package is released when they are declared as complete or ready by the developers. Distributions like Slackware, Debian and CentOS targets in providing the users with the most stable form of operating system which will be attainable as well and also releases the newer versions very frequently. Linux distributions such as Ubuntu and Fedora release its new versions after every six months. Selecting the release cycle which will be perfect for you also depends on various factors. The factors include the software that you require to run, the amount of reliability and stability that you require and the comfort level you are looking out for.

Organizational structure: Although it might not directly affect the distribution performance, it is still one of the most distinguishing factors in between the Linux distributions. Some of the Linux distributions like Gentoo, Debian, Slackware and Arch are all developed by the communities of independent developers while some of the other distributions such as Ubuntu, Fedora and OpenSUSE are developed by those communities which are being sponsored by different corporations. Distribution like CentOS is derived from the distributions which are produced commercially.

Common set of tools: The various distributions of Linux uses different types of tools for performing various common tasks such as configuration of system or management of packages.

Distributions like Ubuntu and Debian uses APT for managing the .deb packages, OpenSUSE uses .rpm package and CentOS along with Fedora also uses .rpm packages but manages all of them by using a tool known as yast. In most of the cases the distribution you choose will end up to that one distribution which comes with all the tools which you require and you are comfortable with. The distributions are designed for performing in different situations. You are required to start with experimenting the distributions for finding out the one that fits you the best according to your need.

Linux Security

When you start using a system based on Linux OS, you become the owner of your system security. The internet is filled up with people who are waiting to use the computing power of your system for satisfying their own goals. Linux offers the users with various security options that help the users in securing their system and tuning the same according to their need.

Finding Your Folders And Files

Everything on a Linux system is in the form of a directory. In Linux, a folder is termed as a directory. Linux OS uses a well-balanced tree of various nested directories for keeping all the files in an organized manner. The directory of the highest level is known as the root directory. It comes designated with only one single slash. In Windows OS, you will come across various drives and disks. But this is not the case in Linux OS. There are several other sub-directories which lie under the root directory. Most of the systems based on Linux come with directories which are called as var and lib along with many others under the tree of the root directory. The directory of lib consists of the system libraries whereas the directory of var consists of all sorts of files which are available in the system which are most likely to change like the mail messages and logs. The directories of Linux OS can also go inside the other directories.

Users and permissions

Linux OS uses a very powerful system for the users and its permissions for making sure that only the right people get access to the system files. As the owner of your Linux system, you can set the users and permissions for every directory. The file access system in Linux comprises of three categories.

Users: A user account is assigned generally to a person or also to an application which requires access to the files in the system. You can provide user access to the system as many numbers you want.

Groups: A group is the collection of one or more than one user. Groups are a great way of granting the same kind of access to various users at one time without the need forsetting permissions for each individually. When you create an account of user, it gets assigned to a default group which comes with the same name as that of the name of the user. A user can be a part of as many groups as the user wants. Users who belong to a
group get all the permissions which are granted for that specific group.

Everyone: This category is for everyone other than the groups and users. When someone accesses the system files without even logging in the system as one specific
user, they fall into the category of everyone. The next important thing that comes right after users is permissions. Each and every directory and file in a Linux system comes with three probable

levels of access.

Read: All the files that come with the permission of read can be viewed.

Write: All the files that come with the permission of write can be edited.

Execute: All the files that come with the permission of execute can be executed or run just like an application. When you start a new script or program, you start executing it.

Software Installation In Linux

Like all the other things in the Linux system, software installation is also done by typing and then executing one specific form of text command. Most of the distributions in Linux come along with managers of package which makes it easier for installing or uninstalling any software in the system. Distributions such as Ubuntu and Debian use APT or the Advanced Packaging Tool package manager whereas CentOS and Fedora use YUM or Yellow-dog Updater Modified manager of packages.

CHAPTER 6: BASIC LINUX COMMANDS

Linux is one of the most famous operating systems that can be found today. However, Linux is not one complete OS, it is the kernel of an OS. Linux is also regarded as a clone of UNIX. Some of the most common distributions of Linux are Linux Mint, Ubuntu Linux, Red Hat Enterprise Linux, Fedora and Debian. Linux is primarily used in the servers. It can also be regarded that almost 90% of the internet is being powered by the servers of Linux. This is mainly because Linux is secure, fast and free as a kernel. Windows servers can also be used for the internet but the main problem that comes with Windows is its costing. This problem of costing can be easily solved by the servers of Linux. In fact, the operating system Android which runs in a majority of the smart-phones today has also been made from the Linux kernel.

Linux Shell

Linux shell is a form of program which receives the commands form the users of a system and transfers it to the operating system for the purpose of processing and then shows the result as well. The Linux shell is the main part of Linux OS. Its distributions come in graphical user interface or GUI but Linux basically comes with command line interface or CLI. For opening up the terminal of Linux shell, you need to press Ctrl+Alt+T in the Ubuntu distribution or you can also press Alt+F2, type in the gnome terminal and then hit enter.

Linux Commands

Let's start with some of the most basic commands of Linux.

pwd

When you open up the terminal first, you will be in the home directory of the user. For knowing exactly in which directory you are in, you can use the command pwd. It helps in giving out the exact path, the path which starts exactly from the root. The root is nothing but the base of the file system in Linux. It is generally denoted by using a forward slash (/). The directory of user generally looks like /home/username.

ls

By using the command ls, you can easily know what are the files within the directory in which you are in. You can also see each and every file which is hidden by using command ls –a.

cd

You can use the command cd for going to a directory. For example, if you are in the folder of home and you wish to go into the folder of downloads, you need to type cd Downloads and you will be in the downloads directory. You need to note that this command is very case sensitive. You are also required to type in the folder name exactly in the way it is in. However, this type of command comes with certain problems. For example, you are having a folder named as Raspberry Pi. In such case, when you enter the command as cd Raspberry Pi, the Linux shell will assume the second argument that comes with the command as a completely different entity and so what you will get in return is only an error message that will say that there is no such directory. In such cases, you can use the backward slash which means use the command as cd Raspberry\Pi. The spaces are taken as : in Linux. If you type the command cd only and hit enter,you will get into the home directory again. In case you want to go back from a specific folder to a folder just before that, you need to use "cd..". The two dots in the command represent the request of going back.

mkdir & rmdir

The mkdir command is being used for the purpose of creating a new folder or directory. For example, when you need to create a new directory such as DIY you need to enter command like mkdir DIY. Always remember that in case you want a directory named as DIY Hacking, you need to type it in as mkdir DIY\Hacking. You can use rmdir command for deleting the directory
which you no longer need. However, always keep in mind that rmdir can only be used at the time of deleting a directory which is empty in nature. If you want to delete one directory which contains files, you need to use rm command.

rm

You can use the command rm for the purpose of deleting the directories and files. If you want to delete the directory only, you need to use rm –r command. When you use the rm command, it will delete the folder along with all the files in it.

touch

This command is used for creating new files. It can be anything, starting from a txt file which is empty to an empty form of a zip file. You can use the command like touch new.txt.

man & - - help

If you want to know in details about a command and how you can use it, you can use the command man. It helps by showing all forms of manual pages of all the commands. For example, if you enter man cd, it will show all the manual pages of the command cd. When you type in the name of the command along with the argument - - help, it will show in which way you can use the command.

cp

The cp command is used for copying files from the command line. It takes in two arguments, the first argument is the file location which is to be copied and the second is where to copy the file.

mv

The command mv is used for moving the files through the line of the command. You can also use this
command for renaming a file. For example, if you need to rename a file "text" to "old" you can type in mv text old. It also takes in

two arguments just like the command cp.

locate

The command locate is used for locating any file in the system of Linux. It is similar to the command of search in the system of Windows. This command might turn out to be very useful when you have no idea where a specific file is located or saved or what is the actual file name. When you use the argument –i with this command, it helps in ignoring the cases. So, for example, if you need to find a file which has the word "bye" in it, it will give out a complete list of all the Linux system files which contains the word "bye" when you use locate –i bye. In case you remember two words from the file name, you can easily separate the two by inserting an
asterisk (*). For instance, for locating a file name with words "bye" and "this", you need to use
locate –i *bye*this.

Intermediate Commands

echo

This command helps in moving some part of data and most of the times text into a file. For instance, if you need to create a brand new text file or add up to the already existing text file, you need to use the command as echo hello, my name is sunny>>new.txt. In this case, you are not required to separate the spaces in a sentence by using \ as in this you will need to put two triangular forms of brackets as you finish with the
writing.

cat

You can use the command cat for displaying all the contents in a file. It is generally used for viewing programs easily.

nano & vi

nano and vid are the text editors which are installed already in the command line if Linux. The command nano is a form of good text editor which helps by denoting the keywords in colors and can also easily recognize most of the languages. The command vi is much simpler in form than nano. By using the command vi, you can create any new file or even modify files by using this form of editor. For instance, you need to create a new file with the name check.txt. You can easily create the same by the use of the command nano check.txt. You can also save the files after you are done with editing by using Ctrl+X and then Y for yes or N for no.

sudo

It is a very widely used command in the system of Linux. The command sudo stands for SuperUser Do. In case you want any of the command to be carried on with the privileges of root or administration, you can use the command sudo. For example, if you need to edit a file such as viz. alba-base.conf, which requires root permissions, you can type in sudo nano alba-base.conf.
You can enter the command line of root by using sudo bash and then type the password of the user. You can also su command for doing the same but you are required to set in one root password before doing that. For setting the password, you need to type sudo passwd and then type in the new password of root.

df

You can use the df command for seeing the disk space which is available in every partition of the system. You just need to type df in the command line and then you can easily view each of the mounted partition along with the available and used space indicated in % along with in KBs. If you want to view the same in megabytes, type in df –m.

du

This command is used for knowing the usage of the disk by a file in the system. In case you are required to know the disk usage for one specific file or folder in the system of Linux, type in du followed by the folder or file name. For example, if you need to know the disk usage which is being used by the folder documents in the system of Linux, type in du Documents. You can also use ls –lah command for viewing the size of the files within a folder.

zip & unzip

You can use the command zip for compressing a file into an archive of zip. For the purpose of extracting files from zip archive use the command unzip.

uname

You can use this command for showing all the information about that system in which your Linux distribution is running. You can type in uname –a for printing the majority of the information about a system.

HARKIRAT SINGH

CHAPTER 7: CHARACTEISTICS OF KALI LINUX AND WHY IT IS SO IMPORTANT

In The Hacking World

Kali Linux is a distribution of Linux which is based on Debian. It has been designed very significantly for the purpose of catering to the needs of the network analysts along with the penetration testers. The wide range of tools that come along with Kali Linux makes it the prime weapon of all the ethical hackers. Kali Linux was previously called Backtrack. Kali Linux is the successor of Backtrack with a more polished version of tools than Backtrack which used to serve the same purpose with a wide range of tools and making the OS jam-packed with several utilities which were not at all necessary. That is why the ethical hackers turned towards Kali Linux which provides tools required for penetration testing in a more simplified form for the ease of functioning.

Why This Os?

Kali Linux comes with a plethora of features. There are also various reasons that justify why one start using Kali Linux should.

Free of cost: Linux is a free software and so all the distributions of Linux are also free of cost. Kali Linux has been and will also be free of cost always.

A wide array of tools: Kali Linux can offer you with more than 600 different types of tools for penetration testing and also various tools related to security analysis.

Open-source software: Linux is an open-source software. So, Kali Linux being a part of the Linux family also follows the much-appreciated model of being open-source. The tree of development of the OS can be viewed publicly on Git and all the codes which are available with Kali Linux are also available for the purpose of tweaking.

Support for multi-language: Although of the fact that the penetration tools are written in English, it is evident that Kali Linux supports multilingual use as well. It has been done to make sure that a greater number of users can operate the OS in their native language and can also locate the tools which they need for their job.

Totally customizable: The developers of the tools for offensive security know that every user will not be agreeing with the model design. So, Kali Linux has been developed in a way so that it can be fully customized according to the need and liking of the user.

System Requirements

Installing Kali Linux for the purpose of penetration testing is very easy. You just need to make sure that you have the required set of hardware. Kali Linux is supported on amd64, i386 and ARM. You all require:

Minimum 20 GB of disk space for the installation of the software

Minimum 1 GB of RAM One CD/DVD drive or virtual box

List Of Tools

Kali Linux comes with a wide range of tools pre-installed. Let's have a look at some of the most commonly used tools.

Aircrack-ng: It is a tools suite which is used for the purpose of assessing Wi-Fi network security. It aims at some of the prime areas of security related to Wi-Fi.

1. Monitoring: It helps in capturing packet and also exports data to the text files for processing in the later stages by the third-party tools.

2. Attacking: It helps in replay attacks, fake access points, de-authentication and various others by the process of packet injection.

3. Testing: It helps in checking the Wi-Fi cards and other capabilities of the drivers.

4. Cracking: It helps in cracking WPA PSK and WEP.

Nmap: Nmap, also known as Network Mapper, it is an open source and free form of utility for the purpose of network discovery along with auditing of security. Nmap uses up the raw packets of IP for determining which hosts are available on the desired network, what are the services are being offered by those hosts, what are the operating systems that they are using, which type of firewall or packet filters are being used and various other characteristics. Many of the administrators of network and systems also use it for:

1. Inventory of network
2. Managing the schedules of service upgrade
3. Monitoring the service or host uptime

THC Hydra: When you are required to crack one remote authentication service, THC Hydra can be used. It is capable of performing super fast dictionary attacks in opposition to 50 or more protocols which includes HTTP, FTP, SMB and HTTPS. It can be used easily for the purpose of cracking into wireless networks, web scanners, packet crafters and many more.

Nessus: It is a form of remote scanning tool which is used for checking the security vulnerabilities of computers. It is not capable of blocking any form of vulnerabilities that the system of a computer has but it can easily sniff all of them out by running more
than 1200 checks for vulnerability and also sends out alerts when it is required to make the security patches.

WireShark: It is an open-source analyzer of packet which anyone can use and that too free of charge. With the help of this tool, the user can easily see the network activities provided along with customizable reports, alerts, triggers and many more.

Features Of Kali Linux

Kali Linux is a form of Linux distribution that comes along with a wide range of tools which are pre-installed in the distribution. It has been designed for the targeted users for ease of functioning. Kali Linux is more or less like the other distributions of Linux but it comes along with some added features too that help in differentiating it from the others. Let's check out some
of the most unique features of Kali Linux.

Live system: Unlike the other distributions of Linux, the primary ISO image that you are going to download will not only help in installing the OS but it can also be used just like a bootable form of live system. In simple words, Kali Linux can be used without even installing it in the system by just using the ISO image by booting the same. The live system of the distribution contains all the tools which are required by the penetration testers. So, in case your present system is not running on Kali Linux OS, you can easily use it by inserting the USB device and then reboot the same for running Kali Linux on your system.

Forensics mode: While performing any kind of forensic related work on the system,generally the users want to avoid any form of activity which might result in data
alteration on the system which is being analyzed. Unfortunately, most of the modernday environments of desktop tend to interfere with this form of objective and tries to auto-mount any form of the disk which it detects. In order to avoid this form of behavior, Kali Linux comes with the forensics mode which can be enabled from the menu of reboot and it will result in disabling all such features. The live system of Kali
Linux turns out to be so useful only for the purpose of forensics as it is readily possible to reboot any system of computer into the system of Kali Linux without even accessing or doing any kind of modification in the hard disks.

Customized Kernel of Linux: Kali Linux is well-known for providing customized version of the recent kernel of Linux which is based on the latest version of Debian
Unstable. This helps in ensuring solid support for hardware, precisely for the wide collection of wireless devices. The kernel of Linux gets patched with the support for wireless injection as some of the assessment tools regarding wireless security tends to rely on this form of feature. As most of the hardware devices need updated files of firmware, Kali Linux comes with the feature of installing the files by default along with
all the firmware updates which are available in the non-free section of Debian.

Trustable OS: The users of this security distribution wants to know that whether or not it can be trusted and as it has been developed plain sight, it allows anyone to easily inspect the codes of the source. Kali Linux has been developed by a very small team of developers who always follow the required practices of security. The developers also upload the source packages in signed format.

Customizable: Each and every penetration tester has their own way of working and might not agree with the default configuration of the OS. Kali Linux is fully
customizable which allows the users to customize the same according to their need.There are also various forms of live-build techniques that can be found online that helpsin modifying the OS, install several other supplementary forms of files, run the arbitrary commands, install any other required packages and many more. The users can also customize the way in which the distribution functions.

CHAPTER 8: INSTALLATION OF KALI LINUX

If you are thinking about pursuing information security for your career, the primary thing that you require is to have an operating system which is focused only on system security. With the help of a proper operating system, you can easily perform various forms of tedious and timeconsuming jobs very easily and efficiently. In the present situation, there are various OS available which are based on Linux. Out of the several distributions that can be found today, Kali Linux is regarded as the best choice for the purpose of information security and penetration testing. It is being widely used by the professional penetration testers and the ethical hackers for performing various activities related to their field along with the assessment of network security.

Kali Linux is regarded as the leading distribution from the house of Linux which is also being used for auditing of security. Kali Linux is the only OS related to ethical hacking and network security that comes pre-packaged with several different types of tools related to the hacking of command line which is required for various tasks related to information security. The tasks in which Kali Linux is most commonly used are application security, penetration testing, forensics related to computer system and security of network. In simple terms, Kali Linux is the one and only and the ultimate operating system which has been designed for the ethical hackers. People who are connected with the world of ethical hacking and penetration testing use Kali Linux for some specific reasons. Kali Linux comes with more than 600 tools for penetration testing. The best part is Kali Linux is 100%

customizable. So, in case you are not liking the present configuration of Kali Linux, you can easily customize it in the way you want. Another

interesting thing about Kali Linux is that it comes with multilingual support. Although the tools are written in English, this allows people from all provinces to use this OS using their own native language. It comes with the support of a wide collection of wireless devices. Kali Linux is such an OS which is developed in a secure form of environment. What makes Kali Linux so popular is the feature of being an open source nature of software which is free as well. It also comes with custom kernel which can also be patched for the purpose of injections.

How Can You Install Kali Linux?

The process of installing Kali Linux in your system is quite easy and simple. The users can also enjoy several options for installing the software. The most preferable options for installation are:

Installation of Kali Linux by using hard disk

Installation of Kali Linux by creating bootable Kali Linux USB Drive

Installing Kali Linux by using software for virtualization like VirtualBox and VMware

Installing Kali Linux by the process of dual booting along with the operating system

The most widely used options for installing Kali Linux are by using USB drive and installation by using VirtualBox or VMware. You need minimum 20 GB of free space in the hard disk of your system along with at least 4 GB of RAM if you are using VirtualBox

or VMware. You will
also require USB along with CD/DVD support.

Installing Kali Linux with the help of VMware

Before you want to run Kali Linux in your system, you will require a virtualization software at the very first place. There are various options available today when it comes to choosing a virtualization software. You can start by installing VMware or VirtualBox from the house of Oracle. After you have installed the virtualization software, you need to launch the same from the folder of applications.Now you are required to download the installation file for Kali Linux which you can easily find from the download page in the official website of Kali Linux. You can choose the one which you think will be meeting your needs. Along with the download file in the download page, you will also come across a wide variety of hexadecimal numbers which are used for the security-related jobs. You are required to check the image integrity which you are going to download. You need to check fingerprint SHA-256 for the file and then compare the same which has been provided on the download page of Kali Linux.After you have downloaded the installation file for Kali Linux, you are required to launch the virtual machine now. For this, you need to open the homepage of VMware Workstation Pro and then select create a new virtual machine. After you have created a new virtual machine, you need to select the iso file of Kali Linux followed by the selection of the guest OS. You will also need to configure all the details of the virtual machine which is Kali Linux in this case. Now you can start the Kali Linux virtual machine simply by selecting the VM for Kali Linux and then selecting the power on button which is green in color. After the virtual machine has powered up, a pop-up menu will be prompted in which you need to select the preferable mode of installation in the GRUB menu. You need to select the option graphical install. Click on continue.The next few screens will be asking you to choose your locale information like the preferred language in which you want Kali Linux to install, the location of your country along with the layout of your keyboard.Once you are done with all the required locale information, the installer will automatically start to install some required additional components for the software and then will also configure the settings related to network. After the components have been installed, the installer will ask you to enter the hostname along with the domain namebfor the purpose of installation. You are required to provide each and every appropriate

 information for proper installation of the software and for continuing with the installation. After you are done with all the above mentioned steps, you will need to set up a password for your machine of Kali Linux and then hit the continue button. Make sure that you do not forget to set a password for your Kali Linux machine. As you set up the password for your Kali Linux machine, the installer will then prompt you for setting up the time zone and will then pause the setup at the time of defining the disk partitions. The installer of the machine will give you four different choices regarding the disk partitions for the machine disk. In case you are not sure about partitioning your disk, the easiest option which is available for you is to select the option of Guided – Use Entire Disk which will be using up the entire disk space and will omit the process of disk partitioning. If you are an experienced user, you can select the option of manual partitioning for more granular options for configuration. You will now require to select the partitioning disk. However, the most recommended option is to select the option for all files in one partition for all the new users. After you gave selected the partitioning disk, select continue.Now you will need to confirm all the changes that you have made to the disk on the machine of the host. Make sure that you do not continue with the process as it will be erasing all the data which is available on the disk. Once you confirm all the changes in the partition, the Kali Linux installer will start running the process of file installation. It might take a while and do not interrupt the process as the system will install everything automatically.

Once all the required files have been installed, the system will be asking you in case you want to set up any network for the purpose of obtaining the future updates and pieces of software. Make sure that you enable this function if you are going to use the repositories of Kali Linux in the future. The system will then configure the manager of package related files.After this step, the system will be asking you to install the boot loader of GRUB. Click on yes and then select the device for writing up the required information of boot loader

to the hard disk which is needed for booting Kali Linux.

Once the installer has finished installing the boot loader of GRUB into the disk, select continue for finishing up the process of installation. It will then install some of the files at the final stage. After you are done with all these steps, Kali Linux will be installed in your system and you can start using the same for the purpose of penetration testing and network security. You can also use Kali Linux in your system by simply creating a USB bootable drive without even installing the

software in the system.

CHAPTER 9: APPLICATIONS AND USE OF KALI LINUX

Kali Linux is a well-known OS in the world of ethical hacking. While it is known that the prime focus of Kali Linux is on the summarized use for penetration testing along with security auditing, Kali Linux can also perform several other tasks apart from these two. Kali Linux has been designed in the form of a framework as it comes with various forms of tools which can cover various types of use cases. Some of the tools of Kali Linux can also be used in combination at the time of performing penetration testing.

For instance, it is possible to use Kali Linux on various types of computers such as on the system of the penetration tester, on the servers of the administrators of the system who wants to monitor their own network, on the systems or workstations of the analysts related to system forensics and also on the embedded form of devices generally along with the ARM CPUs which can be easily dropped in the range of the wireless network or which can also be plugged in the system of the
targeted user. Many of the devices related to ARM also perform as great machines for the purpose of attacking which is mainly because of their small factors of formation along with the requirement very low power.

You can also deploy Kali Linux directly in the cloud for the purpose of quickly building a large farm of machines which are able to crack passwords and on the mobile phones along with tablets for allowing an efficient form of portable testing of penetration.

But it does not end here; the penetration testers also require servers. The servers are required for using a software of collaboration within a large group of penetration testers, for setting up the web server to be used for campaigns related to phishing, for the purpose of running the tools related to vulnerability scanning and for various other interconnected jobs. Once you are done with booting of Kali Linux, you will find out that the main menu of Kali Linux has been organized in accordance to various themes across the different forms of activities
and tasks which are relevant to the penetration testers and other professionals of information security.

Tasks That Can Be Performed With Kali Linux

Kali Linux helps in performing a wide range of tasks. Let's have a look at some of them.

Gathering of information: Kali Linux can be used for collecting various forms of data related to the targeted networks along with the structure of the same. It also helps in identifying the systems of computers, the
operating systems of such computers along with all the services that the computer system runs. Kali Linux can be used for identifying the various potential sensitive parts within the system of information along with the extraction of all forms of listings from the services of a running directory.

Analysis of vulnerability: You can use Kali Linux for the purpose of quick testing of whether a remote or any local system has been affected by any known vulnerabilities or any form of configuration which is not at all secure in nature. The scanners of vulnerability use the databases which contain several signatures for the purpose of identifying the potential threats and vulnerabilities.

Analysis of web application: It helps in the identification of any form of misconfiguration along with weaknesses in the security system of the web applications.

It is a very crucial task to identify and then mitigate such issues given that public availability of such applications makes the same the ideal form of targets for all the attackers.

Assessment of database: Database attacks are the most common form of vector for the attackers that include attacks such as SQL injection to attacks in the credentials. Kali Linux provides various tools which can be used for testing the vector of attacks which ranges from data extraction to SQL injection along with analysis of the same.

Password attacks: The systems connected with authentication are always vulnerable to the attacks of the attackers. A wide array of tools can be found in Kali Linux which ranges from online tools of password attack to the offline tools against the systems of hashing or encryption.

Wireless form of attacks: Wireless networks are pervasive in nature. This means that they are always a common vector of attack for the attackers. Kali Linux comes with a wide range of support related to various cards of the network which makes Kali Linux an obvious choice for the attacks in opposition to the several wireless network types.

Reverse engineering: reverse engineering is a very important form of activity which is being used for various purposes. In providing support for the various forms of offensive activities, reverse engineering is one of the prime methods which is being used for identification of the vulnerabilities and also for tracking the development of exploitation. On the side of defense, it is also being used for analyzing the malware which is employed for the targeted attacks. Within this capacity, the aim is to identify the prime capabilities of a given set of tradecrafts.

Tools for exploitation: Exploitation is the act of taking advantage of any form of existing vulnerability in a system which allows the attacker to gain complete control of a remote form of device or machine. This form of access can also be used by the attackers for further privileges of escalation of attacks which are done either on any form of machine which is accessible to the local network or on the machine which has been compromised. This category of Kali Linux function comes with various tools along with utilities which help in simplifying the overall process writing up your very own form of exploits.

Spoofing and sniffing: Gaining overall access to that packet of data which is travelling across any network is always advantageous for the attackers. Kali Linux can provide you with various tools for the purpose of spoofing which will allow you to imitate any
legitimate user along with the sniffing tools which will allow you to analyze and also capture the available pool of data directly from the network wire. When spoofing as well as sniffing tools are used together, it can turn out to be very powerful.

Post exploitation: Once you have been successful in gaining all-over access to the target system, you might want to maintain the same level of accessibility to the system along with extended control simply by moving laterally over the network. You can find various tools in Kali Linux for assisting you in your goals regarding post exploitation.

Forensics: The live boot environments of Forensic Linux have been very famous in the recent years.Kali

Linux comes with a large number of very popular tools of forensics which are based on Linux which will allow you to perform everything, starting from the initial stage of triage to imaging of data along with full analysis of the system and lastly management of case.

Tools of reporting: A test of penetration can only be declared as successful once all the findings of the test have been properly reported. This category of tools from Kali Linux helps in composing the collected data which has been gathered by the use of tools for information gathering, finding out various non-obvious form of relationships and also bringing together everything in several reports.

Tools for social engineering: When the technical aspect of a system is secured properly, there are chances of exploiting the behavior of human beings as a vector of attack. When provided with the perfect influence, human beings can be induced frequently for taking various actions which ultimately leads to the compromising of the security of a system environment. Did the USB drive which was just now plugged in by the secretary contain any form of harmful PDF? Or did the UDB drive just installed a form of Trojan horse backdoor? Was the website of banking which was used by the accountant just now was a normal expected form of website or a copy of a website for the purpose of phishing attack? Kali Linux comes with various tools that can help you in aiding all these forms of attacks.

Services for system: Kali Linux can provide with tools which will allow you to initiate and also stop various applications which run in the background as the services for the system.

Coordinating Tasks Of Kali Linux

Kali Linux helps in coordinating several tasks and also helps in balancing the coordination between the software and hardware of a system. The first and foremost task of Kali Linux is to control the hardware components of the computer system. It helps in detecting along with figuring out the various hardware components

when the computer turns on or also when any new device is installed. It helps in making the hardware
components available for the various higher level of software with the help of a simplified form of program interface so that the applications can take all-round advantage of the connected devices without the need of addressing any detail like in which extension slot is the option board plugged in. The interface of programming also comes with a layer of abstraction which allows various software to work seamlessly with the hardware.

What Makes Kali Linux Different From Others?

Kali Linux has been specifically designed for gearing up the functioning of the penetration testers and also for the purpose of security auditing. For achieving this, various core changes have also been implemented for Kali Linux which reflects all of these requirements:

Root access by design, single-user: Because of the normal nature of the audits regarding system auditing, Kali Linux has been designed in such a way which can be used in the scenario of single root access. Most of the tools which are employed for the purpose of penetration testing needs escalated form of privileges and as it is typically sound policy for enabling the root privileges when required, during the use cases to which Kali Linux is aimed to, this whole approach might turn out to be a huge burden.

The services of network disabled by default: Kali Linux comes with systematic hooks which disables the services of a network by default. Such hooks allow the users to install several Kali Linux services while also making sure that the distributions also remains completely safe and secure by default no matter which type of packages has been installed. Other additional services like Bluetooth are also kept in the blacklist by
default settings.

Custom kernel of Linux: Kali Linux uses up upstream form of the kernel which is patched for the purpose of wireless injection.

A set of trusted and minimal repositories: The absolute key of Kali Linux is to maintain the integrity of a given system, given all the goals and aims of Kali Linux.
With the prime aim in mind, the complete collection of sources of upstream software which are used by Kali Linux is kept as minimum as possible. Many of the new users of Kali Linux gets tempted to add the extra repositories to the sources.list. But, by doing so, it leads to the risk of breaking the installation of Kali Linux.

It is not correct to suggest that everyone should be using Kali Linux. Kali Linux is been designed particularly for the security specialists. It comes with a unique nature because of which Kali Linux is not a recommended distribution for those who are not at all familiar with the functioning of Linux or are looking out for some general form of Linux distribution for their
desktop, for gaming, designing of website and many more. Even for the experienced users of Linux, Kali Linux might come along with certain challenges which are generally set up due to preserving the security of the systems.

CHAPTER 10: DIFFERENT TOOLS OF KALI LINUX

As we know that Kali Linux is an open source form of distribution which is completely based on Debian, it helps in providing various tools for the purpose of security auditing along with penetration testing. It has been developed by Offensive Security and is also among some of the most well-known distributions and is being widely used by the ethical hackers. The best thing that comes with Kali Linux is that it does not need to be installed as the OS in your system. Instead of that, you can simply run the iso file which can be loaded in the memory of RAM easily for the purpose of testing the security of a system with the help of around 600 tools.

Kali Linux provides users with various forms of tools like information gathering tools, tools for analysis of vulnerability, web application tools, wireless attack tools, tools for forensics, sniffing along with spoofing tools, hardware hacking tool and many more. Let's have a look at some of the most popular tools from Kali Linux.

Tools From Kali Linux

Nmap: Nmap can be regarded as the most popular network mapping tool. It allows the user to find out the active hosts available within a network and also gathers relevant information in relation to penetration testing. Some of the main features of Nmap are:

1. It comes with host discovery and helps in identifying the available network hosts.
2. Nmap comes with the feature of port scanning which allows the users to calculate the total number of open ports on the remote or local form of host.
3. It helps in fetching the OS of a network and also finds out various information about the connected devices.
4. It allows the user to detect the version of the application and also determines the name of the application.
5. It helps in extending the default capabilities of Nmap by the use of NSE or Nmap Scripting Engine.

Netcat: As the name goes by, Netcat functions just like a cat and helps in fetching details about a network. It functions as an application for network exploration which is not only used in the field of security industry but is also famous in the network administration and security administration field. It is generally used for the purpose of checking outbound and inbound network and also for port exploration. It can also be used for conjunction with various languages of programming such as C or Perl or also with bash scripts. The main features of Netcat are:

1. Port analysis of UCP and TDP
2. Sniffing of inbound and outbound network

3. Forward and reverse analysis of DNS
4. Scanning of remote and local ports
5. Integration with the standard input of terminals
6. TCP and UDP tunneling mode

Unicornscan: This is one of the finest tools of infosec which is being used for the purpose of data correction along with gathering. It also offers the users with UDP and TCP scanning along with super beneficial patterns of discovery which helps in finding the remote hosts. It can also help in finding out the software which is running in each of the hosts. The main features of Unicornscan are:

1. Asynchronous scan of TCP
2. Asynchronous scan of UDP
3. Asynchronous banner detection of TCP
4. Application, OS and system service detection
5. Capability of using customized sets of data
6. Supports relational output for SQL

Fierce: Fierce is a tool from Kali Linux which is used for the purpose of port scanning along with network mapping. It can also be used for discovering the hostnames and non-contiguous space of IP across any network. It is somewhat similar in features just like Unicornscan and Nmap but unlike these two, Fierce is specifically being used for the corporate networks. After the target network has been defined by the penetration tester, Fierce runs various tests in opposition to the domain which are selected for retrieving important information which can be used for the further analysis and post
exploitation. The features of Fierce include:

1.Scanning of internal and external IP ranges
2.Capability of changing the DNS server for the purpose of reverse lookup
3.Scanning of IP range and complete Class C

4.Helps in logging capabilities into a file system
5.Discovery of name servers and attack of zone transfer
6.Capabilities of brute force by using the custom list of texts

OpenVAS: Also known as Open Vulnerability Assessment System, is a free software which can be used by anyone for the purpose of exploring the remote or local
vulnerabilities of a network. This tool of security helps in writing and also integrating the customized plugins of security to the platform of OpenVAS. The main features of OpenVAS are:
1.It works as a port scanner and network mapper
2.It helps in discovery of simultaneous host
3.It supports OpenVAS protocol of transfer
4.It comes integrated with databases of SQL such as SQLite
5.It performs weekly or daily scans
6.It helps in exporting the results into HTML, XML or LateX formats of files
7.It comes with the capability of resuming, pausing and stopping the scans
8.It is fully supported by both Linux and Windows

Nikto: Nikto is written in Perl and is a tool which is included in Kali Linux, it works as a complementary tool to OpenVAS and to other tools of vulnerability scanner. It allows the penetration testers along with the ethical hackers to carry on with scanning of a full web server for the discovery of vulnerabilities along with flaws in security. This tool gathers all the results of security scanning by finding out the insecure patterns of
application and files, server software which has
become outdated and the default names along with misconfiguration of software as well as of server. It also supports various proxies for SSL encryption, authentication based on host and many others. The main
features of Nikto are:

1.It helps in scanning multiple ports which are

available on a server

2.It comes with evasion techniques of IDS

3.It provides the output results in XML, TXT, NBE, HTML and CSV

4. It comes with the enumeration of Apache and cgiwrap username

5. It performs scans for the specified directories of CGI

6. It can identify the software which is installed in the system via the files, favicons

and headers

7. It uses up custom files of configuration

8. It helps in debugging and providing verbose output

WPScan: WPScan is used for the purpose of auditing the installation security of WordPress. With the help of WPScan, you can easily find out whether or not the setup of your WordPress is susceptible to any form of attack or not or whether if it is giving out too much information in the core, theme files or plugins. This tool also allows the users to find the weak passwords for each and every registered user and can also run a brute force attack for finding out which one can be cracked. The features of WPScan are:

1. Enumeration of WP username

2. Security scans of non-intrusive nature

3. Enumeration of WP plugin vulnerability

4. Cracking of weak password and brute force attack of WP

5. Scheduling of WordPress security scans

CMSMap: CMSMap is an open source form of project which is written in Python. It helps in automating the task of vulnerability scanning along with detection in Joomla,WordPress, Moodle and Drupal. This tool can also be used for running a brute force attack and also for launching the various exploits once the vulnerabilities have been discovered. The main features of CMSMap are:

1.It supports multiple threats scan

2.It comes with the capability of setting customized header and user agent

3.It supports encryption of SSL

4.It saves the output file in the form of text file

Fluxion: This tool functions as an analyzer of Wi-Fi which specializes in attacks of MITM WPA. It allows the users to easily scan the wireless form of networks, search for any form of security flaw in the personal or corporate networks. Unlike the other tools for Wi-Fi cracking, this tool does not perform any form of brute force attack for cracking attempt as it takes generally a lot of time. Instead of launching a brute force attack, this tool spawns a process of MDK3 which makes sure that all the users who are connected with the targeted network are deauthenticated. After this has been done, the user gets a prompt screen for connecting with a fake pint of access where they are required to enter the Wi-Fi password. Then the tool sends the password of Wi-Fi to you so that you can easily gain access to the same. Other than all these tools, there are several other tools from Kali Linux such as Aircrack-ng, Kismet Wireless, Wireshark, John the Ripper and many others.

CHAPTER 11: HOW CAN KALI LINUX BE USED FOR HACKING?

As we all know by now that Kali Linux has been designed especially for the purpose of penetration testing and security auditing, it can also be used for the purpose of ethical hacking which is required while performing penetration testing and other security checks. Kali Linux comes packed with a huge number of tools which helps in the venture of security infrastructure testing and other forms of testing for securing an organization or company.

Who all uses Kali Linux and why?

Kali Linux can be regarded as the most unique form of OS which can be found today as serves as a platform which can be used up by both the good guys and the bad guys. The administrators of security along with the black hat hackers all use this platform for meeting their needs. One uses this system for the purpose of preventing and detecting breaches in security infrastructure while the other uses this OS for identifying and thereby exploiting the security breaches. The huge number of tools which comes packed with Kali Linux can be regarded as the Swiss Knife for the toolbox of the security professionals. The professionals who widely use Kali Linux are:

Security Administrators: The administrators of security come with the responsibility of safeguarding the information and data of the concerned institution. The security administrators widely use Kali Linux for the purpose of ensuring that there are no forms of vulnerabilities in the environment of the security infrastructure.

Network administrators: The network administrators come with the responsibility of maintaining a secure and efficient network. Kali Linux is used by the network administrators for the purpose of auditing of network. For instance, Kali Linux can easily detect the access points of rogue.

Architects of network: Such people are responsible for the designing of a secure environment for a network. They use Kali Linux for auditing the internal network designs and makes sure that nothing has been misconfigured or overlooked.

Penetration testers: The penetration testers use Kali Linux for auditing the security environments and also perform reconnaissance for the corporate environments which they are bound to take care of.

CISO: The Chief Information Security Officer takes help of Kali Linux for the purpose of internal auditing of the environment of their infrastructure and finds out if any new form of application or configurations of rogue has been installed in the environment.

Forensic engineers: Kali Linux comes along with a mode of forensics which allows the forensic engineers for performing discovery of data along with data
recovery in various instances.

White hat hackers: The white hat hackers or the ethical hackers are similar to the penetration testers who use Kali Linux for auditing and for finding out vulnerabilities which might be present within a security
environment.

Black hat hackers: The black hat hackers use Kali Linux for finding out vulnerabilities in a system and then exploiting the same. Kali Linux comes with various applications of social engineering which can be easily used by the black hat hackers for compromising an individual or an organization.

Grey hat hackers: The grey hat hackers also use Kali Linux just like the black hat as well as the white hat hackers.

Computer enthusiasts: It is a very generic form of term but any person who is interested in getting to know more about computers and networking can use the system of Kali Linux for the purpose of learning more about networking, information technology and common form of vulnerabilities.

Process Of Hacking

Kali Linux is very popular as a hacking platform. The word "hacking" might not always be negative as it is also being used for various other jobs other than exploitation. By gathering immense knowledge about the process of hacking with Kali Linux, you can learn how to perform for vulnerability check and how to fix them as well in case you want to choose ethical hacking as

your career option. The process of hacking with Kali Linux is similar to that of a general hacking process in which a hacker tries to get into the server of an organization or company and thereby gain all forms of access to the data which is stored in the servers. The process of hacking can be divided into five different steps.

Reconnaissance: This is regarded as the very first step while starting with the process of hacking. In this step, the hacker tends to use all the available means for the purpose of collection of all forms of information about the targeted system. It includes various phases such as target identification, determining the target IP address range, available network, records of DNS and many others. In simple terms, the hacker gathers all contacts of a website or server. This can be achieved by the hacker by using various forms of search engines like maltego, researching about the system of the target, for

instance, a server or website or by utilizing various other forms of tools like HTTPTrack for the purpose of downloading a complete website for enumeration at

later stages. After the hacker is done with all these steps, he can figure out the employee names, the positions of the employees along with the designated email

addresses of the employees.

Scanning: After the collection of all forms of information regarding the target, the hacker starts with the second phase which is scanning. The hackers utilize several forms of tools in this phase such as dialers, port scanner, network mappers, scanners of vulnerability and many others. As Kali Linux comes pre-loaded with a huge bunch of tools, the hackers won't even face any form of difficulty during this phase. The hackers try to find out that information about the target system which can actually help in moving ahead with an attack such as IP addresses, the accounts of the users and computer names. As the hackers get done with basic information collection, they start looking out for the other possible avenues of attack within the target system. The hackers can select various tools from Kali Linux for the purpose of network mapping such as Nmap. The hackers try to find out automated email reply system or simply by basing on the information which has been gathered by them. The hackers move to the next step which includes emailing the staffs of the company regarding various queries, such as mailing the HR of a company about a detailed enquiry on job vacancy.

Gaining overall access: This phase is regarded as the most important of all when it comes to hacking. In this phase, the attacker attempts to create the design of the
network blueprint which has been targeted. It is created with all the relevant information which has been collected by the hacker. After the hackers finish the phase of enumeration and scanning, the step that comes now is gaining access of the targeted network which is based completely on the information collected. It might happen that the hacker wants to use phishing attack. He might try to take it safe and thus use only a very simple attack of phishing for the purpose of gaining access. The hacker can decide to get into the targeted system from the IT department of the organization. The attacker might also get to know that some recent hiring has been done by the company and it can help in speeding up the procedure. For the phishing attack, the hacker might send out emails of phishing by using the actual address of email of the CTO of the company with the use of a unique form of program and will send out the mails to all the technicians. The email which will be used for the purpose of phishing will be containing a website which will help in gathering all the required user ids and passwords for the purpose of logging in. The hacker can also use other choices like phone app, website mail or some other platform for the purpose of sending out mail of phishing to the users and then asking the individuals for logging in to a new Google portal with the use of their provided credentials. When the hackers decide to

use such a technique, they have a special type of program which runs in the background in their system which is called Social Engineering Toolkit. It is used by attackers for sending out the emails with the address of the server to the users directly after masking the server address with the help of bitly or tinyurl. The attackers can also use other methods for gaining access to the system such as by making a reverse TCP/IP shell in the PFD format file which can be created by the use of Metasploit. The attackers can also employ overflows of buffer for the attacks which are based on stacking or hijacking of the sessions which ultimately results in gaining overall access to the targeted server.

Maintaining the access to the server: After the hacker has gained access to the target server, he will try to keep the access to the server as it is and keeping it safe for future exploitation and attacks. When a hacker gets access to an overall system, he can use the system as his own personal base and use the same for launching several other attacks to the other systems. After a hacker gains access to a targeted system and ultimately owns the same, the hijacked system is called a zombie system. The hacker gains access to a whole new array of email addresses and accounts and can start using those for testing other form attacks right from the same domain. For the purpose hiding in the system, the hacker also tries to create a brand new administrator account and tries to get dissolved in the system. For safety purposes, the hacker also starts to find out and identify those accounts in a system which has not been used by the organization for a long period of time. After the hacker finds out such form of accounts, he changes all the login passwords of the old accounts and elevates all form of privileges right to the administrator of the system like a secondary account for the purpose of having safe access to the network which has been targeted. The hacker can also begin to send out various emails to the other users within an organization which might contain exploited form of files in the PDF format with the reverse shell scheme for extending his allround access within the system. After all these, the hacker waits for some time to make sure that no form of disturbance has been detected in the system and after getting sure of the same, he starts to create copies of the available pool of user data like contacts, files, messages, emails and various other forms of data for using them in the later stage.

Clearance of track: Before starting a system attack, the hackers plans out their whole pathway for the attack along with their planning for identity so that if any discrepancy occurs no one can trace them up. The hackers start doing so by altering their MAC address and then run the same system across a VPN so that their identity can be covered up easily. After the hackers have achieved their target, they begin with clearance of their pathways and tracks. This complete phase includes various things such as clearing of the temp files, mails which has been sent, the logs of the servers and various other things. The hacker also tries to make sure that there is no form of alert message from the email provider which can alarm the targeted organization regarding any form of unauthorized or unrecognized login in the system. A penetration tester follows all these steps for the purpose of testing the vulnerabilities of a system and making sure that those which are available in the system are mended properly.

CHAPTER 12: TECHNIQUES OF PORT SCANNING USING KALI LINUX

Identification of the open ports on the targeted system is essential for defining the surface of attack of the target. The open ports of the target correspond with the networked services which are running on the system. Errors in programming or flaws in implementation can result in making all these services very much susceptible to the attacks and can also lead to compromise

of the overall system. For the purpose of determining the most probable vectors of attack, you are required to enumerate all the ports which are in open condition on all the systems of remote form within the scope of the project. The open number of ports also corresponds with the services which can be easily addressed with the help of either TCP or UDP traffic. Both UDP and TCP are protocols of transport. TCP or Transmission Control Protocol is the one which is more commonly used than UDP and also provides communication which is connectionoriented. UDP or User Datagram Protocol is a protocol which non-connection oriented in nature

which is also sometimes used along with the services in which transmission speed is more important than the integrity of data. The form of penetration testing which used for the purpose of enumerating such services is known as port scanning. Such technique helps in yielding enough amount of information for the purpose of identifying whether the service is being associated with any port on the server or on the device.

Udp Port Scanning

As TCP is more frequently used than UDP as a protocol 0f transport layer, services which are operated by UDP are most often forgotten. In spite of the normal tendency of overlooking the services of UDP, it is also critical for these services to be enumerated for acquiring an overall understanding of the surface of attack of any form of target. The form of scanning with UDP might often turn out to be tedious, challenging and time-consuming as well. For gaining overall insight into the functioning of these tools it is very essential to understand the two exactly different approaches of UDP scanning which is used.

The first technique which is used is to rely on the ICMP port unreachable responses exclusively. This form of scanning relies on those assumptions which the UDP ports which are not linked with the live service will return ICMP port unreachable response. Lack of this response is taken as the indication of a live form of service. Although this form of approach might turn out to be very effective in various circumstances, there are also chances of the same of returning inaccurate form of results in the cases in which the host is unable to generate port unreachable response or the replies of port unreachable is either filtered by any form of firewall or are rate limited.

It also comes with an alternative in which service specific probes are used for attempting soliciting of a response which will indicate that the service which was expected is running on the port which is targeted. Although this form of approach might turn out to be very effective, it is also very time-consuming at the same time.

Tcp Port Scanning

TCP port scanning includes various approaches such as connect scanning, stealth scanning along with zombie scanning. For understanding how all these techniques of scanning work, you need to understand how the connections of TCP are established and also maintained. TCP is a form of protocol which is connection-oriented. Data is transported over TCP only after a successful

connection has been created in between the two systems. The process which is associated with the creation of connection of TCP is often called three-way handshake. This term alludes from the three different steps which are involved in the process of connection. A packet of TCP SYN is sent from that device which wants to establish connection along with the device port which it wants to connect with. If the associate service with the port which the device wants to connect to accepts the connection, the port will be replying to the system which is requesting the connection with a packet of TCP that comes with both ACK and SYN bits

activated. The connection is successful when the requesting system responds back to the port with a response of TCP ACK. These three steps in total sums up the three-step process which is required for the establishment of a session of TCP between two systems. All the techniques of TCP port scanning will be performing some sort of variation of this entire process for the

purpose of identifying the live services on the remote form of hosts. Both the process of stealth scanning and connect scanning are quite easy to understand. The

process of connect scanning is used up for establishing a complete TCP connection every port which is being scanned. This is done for each of the ports which are scanned for completing the three-way handshake. When a connection is established successfully, the port is determined to be in the open state. However, in the case of stealth scanning, a full connection is not established. Stealth scanning is often referred to as SYN scanning or also half open scanning. For each and every port which are scanned, one single packet of SYN is sent out to the port of destination and all the ports which replies with a packet of SYN+ACK are taken as to be running the live form of services. As no final form of ACK is sent out from the system which initiated the connection, the connec-

tion is left out as half open. This is known as stealth scanning as the solutions of logging which only records the connections which are established do not record any form of evidence of the performed scan. The final method which comes with TCP scanning is the zombie scanning. The prime goal of
zombie scanning is to map all the open form of ports on a system of remote nature without even producing any form of evidence which you have had an interaction with the system. The principles on which the functioning of zombie scanning depends are complex in nature. You can carry out zombie scanning by following these steps.

Start by identifying the remote system for the zombie. The system which you are going to identify needs to have these characteristics:
1. It is in idle form and it doesn't actively communicate with the other systems
which are available on the network.
2. It needs to use an incremental form of IPID sequence.
Then you will need to send in a packet of SYN+ACK to the zombie and then record the initial value of IPID.

Send in a packet of SYN along with a source of the spoofed IP address of the system of zombie to the target system of scan. Depending on the port status on the target scan, any of the following will happen:

1. In case the port is in open state, the scan target will be returning a packet of SYN+ACK to the host of zombie which it thinks sent out the original request of SYN. In such a case, the host of zombie will be responding to the unsolicited form of SYN+ACK packet with a packet of RST and then increment the value of IPID by one.
2. In case the port is in the closed state, the scan target will be returning a response of RST to the host of zombie which it thinks sent out the original request of SYN.
The packet of RST will be soliciting no form of response from

the host of zombie and the value of IPID will therefore not be increased. Send in another packet of SYN+ACK to the host of zombie and then evaluate the final value of IPID of the RST response which has been returned. In case the value has been increased by one,

the port on the target scan is closed and in case the value has been increased by two the port on the target scan is in open state. For performing a zombie form of scan, an initial request of SYN/ACK is required to be sent to the system of zombie for the purpose of determining the current value of IPID within the returned packet of RST. A spoofed packet of SYN is then sent out to the scan target along with a form of source IP address of the system of zombie. As the zombie actually did not send out the initial request of SYN, it will be interpreting the response of SYN/ACK as being unsolicited and then send a packet of RST back to the system of target and thus increasing the value of IPID by one. At the final stage, another packet of SYN/ACK needs to be sent to the system of zombie which will return a packet of RST and then increase the value of IPID by one.

CHAPTER 13:PENETRATION TESTING

Each and every infrastructure of IT comes with some weak points which can ultimately lead to some serious attack and can be used for the purpose of stealing and manipulating data. Only one thing can be done in such situations which can help in preventing the hackers from entering the system. You need to perform regular checks of the infrastructure of your security and make sure that there is no form of vulnerabilities present in the structure. Penetration testing helps in finding out the vulnerabilities along with the several weak points in a system. As the owner or administrator of a network, they can always have some advantage over the hackers as they are bound to know the topology of network, the components of infrastructure, the services, the probable points of attack, the executed services and many more. Penetration testing is done within a real and secure environment so that in case any vulnerability is found, you can mend the same and secure the system.

Penetration testing in details

As the name goes by, penetration testing is the process of testing a system to find out whether penetration by any third party is possible in the system or not. Penetration testing is often mixed up with ethical hacking as both are somewhat similar in features and functioning. The motive of are also the same but a very thin line differentiates the two. In penetration testing, the tester scans for any form of vulnerability in the system, malicious form of content, risks and flaws in the concerned system. Penetration testing can be performed either in an online network or server or a computer system as well. Penetration testing comes with the goal of strengthening the security system of an organization for the motive of properly defending the security of a system. Unlike hacking, penetration testing legal in

nature and is done with all forms of official workings. If used in the proper way it can do wonders. Penetration testing can be considered as a significant

❖ ❖ ❖

Part Of Ethical Hacking

Penetration testing needs to be performed at regular intervals as it comes with the power of improving the capabilities of a system and also improves the strategies related to cyber security. Various types of malicious content are created for the purpose of fishing out the weak points which are available within a program, application or system. For effective testing, the

malicious content which is created is spread across the entire network for vulnerability testing. The process of penetration testing might not be able to handle all the concerns related to security; however, it can help in minimizing the probable chances of any form of attack. It helps in making sure that a company is safe from all forms of vulnerabilities and thus protecting the same from cyber attacks. It also helps in checking whether or not the defensive measures are enough for the organization and which of the security measures are required to be changed for the motive of decreasing the vulnerability of the system. Penetration testing is really helpful in pointing out the strengths along with

the weaknesses in the structure of an organization at any one given point of time. You need to note that this whole process if not at all casual in nature. It includes rigorous planning, granting of the required permissions from the concerned management and then
initiating the process.

Security scanners

The process of penetration testing starts after an overview of the complete organization has been collected and then the process of searching for the specific weak points starts. For performing all these, you are required to use a security scanner. Depending on the type and nature of the security scanners, the tools can actually help in checking an entire system or network for the weak points which are known. One of the most comprehensive forms of tool for security scanning is OpenVAS. This tool comes with the idea of a huge number of vulnerabilities and can also check for the defenses. After the OpenVAS tool has identified all the open form of tools, you can easily use Nmap for discovering the details. A tool like Wireshark will allow you to find
out any form of content which is critical in nature along with any critical form of network activity which can point out certain patterns of attack.nThe classic form of Wireshark tool is also useful in identifying the bottlenecks which can indicate the attacks of the hackers and also requires a continuous check. In the world of corporate organizations, the applications which are based on the web often depend on MySQL, Apache and
stack of PHP. All these platforms dominate the entire landscape. Such platforms are the favorite targets of the hackers as they usually come with great opportunities of attacks. Kali Linux comes with around two dozen tools which specialize in web application testing. Such scanners can be easily found in the menu of Web Application Analysis. The w3af and Burp Suite are regarded as the best tools of the lot.

Burp Suite helps in the identification and testing of the vulnerabilities and is quite easy to use. Brute force attack can be launched from the module of the intruder which takes help of the request records which are grouped in the proxy intercept tab for the purpose of injecting the required payload in the system of the web. It also helps in detecting configurations of poor
security. Configuration of incorrect nature of the security settings can take place at any of the levels of the stack of application. For the purpose of detecting these vulnerabilities, Burp Suite starts with the identification of the target and then executes the Spider command from the menu of context. The outputs which can be found from the scans can help you in finding out the
misconfigurations in the system. Generally, a great amount of caution is needed at the time of product system analyzing with the security scanners which are not designed in a way for getting handled by the kid hands. Although various actions serve for identifying the points of attack, you can expect that the concerned
system which is being tested might also get affected. So, you are required to perform all these tests within mirrored form of systems. Generally, the mirrors of the systems are secured by the firewall and IDSs of the system of production, so you can also check the overall effectiveness of the protection mechanisms which are existing already. Several forms of tools can run in various modes which might make it difficult for the IDSs to properly detect the scans. While running in the intelligent modes, they often fail to get detected.

Sounding the weak points

After you have found out where are the gaps in the, the next step that you need to perform is to sound all of them out. An important portion of the penetration tests is the use of the tools which helps in stimulating as many patterns of attack as possible. Metasploit can be regarded as the most widely used form of tool for penetration testing and is also a great tool for the penetration testers.

CHAPTER 14: VPN

VPN or virtual private network is the method of connection which is used for adding privacy along with security to any public or private form of network like the internet or hotspots of Wi-Fi. VPNs are most widely used by the corporations for the purpose of protecting various forms of private and sensitive data. However, in the recent years, the craze of using private VPNs is
increasing day by day. This is mainly because of the fact that all those interactions which were face to face in the beginning now transformed to the internet form of communication. Privacy increases with the use of VPN as the IP address of the initial system get replaced with the IP address which is provided by the provider of a virtual private network. The subscribers can get an IP address from any city they want from the provider of VPN service. For example, you are living in San Francisco but with service provided by virtual private network, you can look like that you live in Amsterdam, London or any other city.

Security

Security is the prime reason for which the corporations have been using the services of VPNs for years. There are various simple ways on which data can traveling to a network can be intercepted. Firesheep and Wi-Fi spoofing are the two easiest ways in which information can be hacked. For a better understanding of the concept of VPN, a firewall helps in protecting a system along with data on the computer while a VPN helps in protecting all forms of data on the internet or on the web. VPNs cater with the help of various advanced forms of encryption protocols and techniques of tunnel security for the purpose of encapsulating all the transfers of online data. The most computer savvy users will never connect to the internet without a proper firewall and updated system of antivirus. The evolving number of security threats along with the increase of reliance on the internet, it has made virtual private network a very important part of a well-designed security infrastructure. The checks of integrity ensure that no form of data is lost along with ensuring that the connection which has been established is not hijacked. As all the traffic gets protected, VPNs are always preferred more than the proxies.

Setting up a VPN

The setting up of a VPN is a pretty simple job. It is most often as easy as entering the username and password. The dominant nature of smartphones can easily configure VPNs by using the L2TP/IPsec and PPTP protocols. All forms of major OS can configure VPN PPTP connection. L2TP/IPsec and OpenVPN protocols need a small application which is of open source nature and the certifications to be separately downloaded.

Protocols of VPN

The available pool of protocols along with the features of security tends to grow with the flow of time. The most widely found protocols are:

PPTP: This form of protocol has been in the world of VPN since the early days of Windows 95. The major advantage of PPTP is that it can be easily set up on any form of major OS. In simple words, PPTP helps in tunneling point to point connections over the protocol of GRE. However, the security concerning PPTP has been recently called out into several questions but it is strong enough although it is not the one which is the most secure of all.

L2TP/IPsec: L2TP/IPsec is much more secure when compared with PPTP and it also comes with several other features. L2TP/IPsec is the method of implementing two different types of protocols all together in proper order for gaining the overall features of all. For instance, the protocol of L2TP is being widely used for creating tunnel and IPsec protocol helps by providing a secure form of channel. These features of the protocols make them a highly secure form of package.

OpenVPN: OpenVPN is a virtual private network which is based on SSL and is gaining popularity day by day. The software which is being used for this protocol is open source in nature and is also highly available. SSL is a form of mature protocol concerned with encryption. OpenVPN can easily run on any single TCP or UDP port and thus makes this extremely flexible in nature.

How can VPN help?

The concept behind the working of a VPN is quite simple. It helps in connecting PC, smartphone or any other form of device with another computer or server directly on the platform of the internet. It also allows users to surf the contents which are available on the internet by using the same internet connection of the computer. So, when the computer system with which you are connecting to for the purpose of internet surfing is from some other country or region, it will be

showing that the user who is connecting is also from the similar country as the server. So, VPN can actually help you in connecting with all those sites with which you normally can't. You can use VPN for several tasks such as: Bypassing all the restrictions on those websites whose access are restricted only according to geography, mainly for the purpose of streaming audio and video. It can help in protecting the users while connecting to any form of unknown Wi-Fi hotspot. You can watch online streaming of media directly with the help of VPN such as Netflix and Prime.You can gain a considerable amount of privacy online as VPN helps in hiding the actual location of your system. It can help you by protecting your system from scans at the time of using torrent. The use of VPN today is mostly found for bypassing the restrictions on geography for the motive

of watching various forms of restricted contents on the internet simply by taking into use the network of some other torrent or country. It is really helpful at the time of accessing public form of Wi-Fi like the ones which can be found at the coffee shops.

How can you get a VPN for yourself?

Getting a VPN is not that tough and you can get it for yourself depending on your needs. You can start by creating a VPN server for yourself or you can also VPN server. In case you want to create a VPN for your workplace you can do that as well. However, in most of the cases, the use of VPN can be found for the surfing of those contents which are restricted according to the geography of an area such as for torrent which has been banned for many regions and countries. You can download VPN online if you require it only for bypassing the restrictions.
How does VPN work?

When you connect any device such as tablet, smartphone or PC with the VPN, your system of device will start imitating like the local network of the VPN. The traffic of the network will be sent through a secure form of connection directly to the VPN. As the system of the user starts behaving like it is from the same network, the user can easily access all the resources from the local network when the user is seating at some other point of the world. You can also use VPN for imitating as if you are at the same location as of the VPN network. Such a feature gets into play at the time of accessing the websites which are geo-restricted. As you start surfing the internet after getting connected with your desired VPN, your device will be establishing connection with the website through the connection of the VPN which stays encrypted throughout the connection. The VPN will be carrying forward your request to the website server and will also bring back the response via the same channel.

VPN and its uses

VPN has turned out to be a hot topic in the recent years, especially after the restriction of various websites and contents according to the geography of an area. VPN can be used for various jobs. Let's have a look at some of the most basic uses of VPN. You can access your business network at any time while you are on the move. VPN is being used by all the travelers who need to travel around for the purpose of business. Such people need to access the resources of their business network. VPN can be used for business network access along with access of the local network resources at the time of travelling. The local network resources are not needed to be exposed to the internet directly and thus it helps in improving the all-round security of the connection. You can also use VPN for accessing your home-based network while you are travelling. For this, you will need to create a VPN for accessing your personal network
while travelling. This will allow you to access a kind of remote

desktop access which is possible directly over the internet with the use of VPN. The users can use this feature for sharing the local area files, for playing online games by imitating that your device is also on the similar network as of the VPN. You can use VPN for hiding your activities of browsing along with ISP. Suppose you are using a Wi-Fi network which is public in nature. When you browse anything by using such network, the websites which are not of HTTPS nature will be easily

available for all those users who are also using the same network in case they know how to carry on such activities. While using public Wi-Fi, it is always safe to hide all your activities of browsing as it also provides a great amount of privacy on the network. VPN can be used for such purposes. Anything that you request over the internet will be passing through the VPN connection and thus providing you great amount of privacy. This technique is also useful for the purpose of bypassing the connection monitoring by the ISP. VPN is widely used today for the purpose of bypassing of censorship which can be found widely over the internet. With the use of VPN, you can use the firewall of the local area network and then access the internet with the firewall of the VPN network. You can browse all those websites which are geo-blocked with the help of VPN. VPN

can help in easily accessing all those websites which are restricted for several regions and countries. You can also use VPN for watching online streaming of media when you are not in your country like Hula, Netflix and several others. VPN is also used for file transfers.

CHAPTER 15: FIREWALL

As the rate of cyber crime tends to increase day by day which has turned out to be a threat for most of the businesses all over the world, firewall security is the ultimate thing that can help for securing your organization. The term firewall can actually be compared with a physical form of wall which can help in preventing all forms of unwanted parties across it. Firewall security in the world of computer works like a network device which helps in blocking various forms of network traffic and thus creates a huge barrier between the untrusted and trusted form of networks. It is also relatable to the physical walls in the sense that it tries to block the spread of computer attacks.

Firewall And Its Types

With the increase in the percentage of cyber attacks, the types of firewall are also evolving with time. There are several types and forms of firewalls that can be found today. Let's have a look at some of them.

Stateful firewall

Stateful firewall is a type of firewall which is somewhat intelligent by nature. It helps in keeping a detailed track of all the connections which are in the active state to make sure that the

user can easily customize the firewall management rules in a way which will allow the return packets which are in real a part of the established form of connection. However, this form of wall cannot
differentiate in between the bad and good form of network traffic. It comes with prevention form intrusion followed by a complete blockage of the harmful web attacks.

Packet filtering firewall

This form of firewall is somewhat similar to that of the stateful firewall. It comes with various rules for the security of firewall and it comes with the capability of blocking that traffic of internet which is based on the port numbers, IP addresses and IP protocol. The only bad thing about this type of firewall is that it allows all forms of network traffic including the ones which can actually call about an attack. In such cases, the users of such firewall require intrusion prevention with firewall security. By this method, it will be able to filter out the bad and good web traffic. Packet filtering firewall cannot also differentiate between the authentic form of
return packet and the one which imitates the actions of a legitimate data packet. So, it is evident that the packet filtering form of firewall will be allowing all forms of return packets within your network.

Application-aware firewall

This form of firewall is capable of understanding the different forms of protocols and also defines the same for the purpose of addressing the particular sections of the protocol by the signatories or rules. It helps by providing a flexible form of firewall protection for the systems of computers. It also permits the rules to be both particular and comprehensive at the same time. It helps in improving the overall functioning of the deep packet form of inspection, however, there are certain types of attacks which might not be noticed by this firewall because the routines defining of the firewall is not strong enough for managing the actual traffic variations.

Deep packet inspection

This is a type of firewall which helps in examining the packets of data in real. It also looks after the types of attacks over the application layer. This type of firewall comes with the capability of performing various functions in relation to the prevention of intrusion. This form of firewall comes along with three forms of different admonitions. At first, the definition of deep inspection might extend to particular depth for some of the vendors within the data packets and thus will not be examining the entire data packet. This can also conclude in skipping out some of the most dangerous

forms of attacks. Secondly, this type of firewall depends greatly on the form of hardware. So, the hardware
involved in a system might not come with the required power of processing the deep inspection of the data packets. You will need to ensure the capacity of bandwidth which the firewall can manage easily while inspecting the packets. Lastly, the technology which is related to the firewall management might not be
having the needed percentage of flexibility for
managing all the attacks.

Application proxy firewall

This form of firewall might perform as the mediator for various forms of applications like HTTP or the web traffic which intercepts each and every request. It also validates each of them just before allowing them entry. This form of firewall comes with some prime features of intrusion prevention. It is, however, difficult to apply this type of firewall in its complete state. Each of the proxies can handle only one protocol just like the incoming form of web or email. In order to get the ultimate protection of this firewall, it is required to accept all the protocols for the purpose of getting ahead with the protocol violation blocking.

Firewall Security And Its Importance

In this world of today where cyber attacks can take place any time, firewall security is of utmost importance for all the servers and computer systems. The prying eyes are always looking around for the susceptible form of devices which remains connected with the internet. The devices which connect with the internet can be easily attacked by the hackers by implementing any form of harmful code or malware into the device via the gateway of the internet. Malware attack can result in breaching of data and exploitation as well. Firewall is really important in such situations as:

It helps in protecting the systems of computers from all forms of unauthorized access.

It helps in identifying harmful content and also blocks the same.

It helps in establishing a secure working environment for a network which gets used by several people at one time.

It helps in protecting all types of confidential and personal data

◆ ◆ ◆

CHAPTER 16: CRYPTOGRAPHY

With a sudden increase in the percentage of cyber attacks, it is has turned out to be really important to protect all sorts of sensitive data to the maximum extent as possible. Leakage of data in this world of today might result in some serious losses for many of the businesses or might also result as a threat for someone individual like stealing bank details, credit card details, login ids and passwords and many more. Cryptography is the process which is which to convert simple and plain text into a form which is unintelligible in nature. This technique makes the task of storage as well as transmission of confidential data super easy. Cryptographic texts can only be read by that person who is meant to get the message and read the same. It helps in data protection as well as in authentication of data. Cryptography is often linked with the security of all sorts of information which also includes the techniques for communication and those which are derived from the mathematical concepts. The technique uses a particular set of rules along with calculations which arc also called algorithms. They are used for message transformation into such a form that it turns out to be super tough to decipher the message. The algorithms are also used for key generation of cryptography along with digital form of signing for the purpose of data privacy, securing website browsing and for the sensitive forms of communication such as credit card transactions, bank details and email.

Cryptography And Its Techniques

The technique of this process is also linked along with features of

cryptology and cryptanalysis. The technique uses various other techniques which include words merging with pictures, usage of mircodots and various other steps which helps in hiding out the information which is to be transported over a network or is meant to be stored in the same. The plain form of text is converted into a coded form of text which is often called cipher-text. It is done with the process of
encryption. It can be deciphered with the process of decryption at the receiver end.

Cryptography And Its Objectives

Cryptography comes with various objectives. Let's have a look at them. Cryptography comes with the goal of maintaining data integrity. The piece of information or data which is to be transmitted between the sender and the receiver or which is meant to be stored in the network cannot be altered or changed in any way. In any case, if such things happen, both the parties in communication get notified. It also comes with the objective of protecting all forms of sensitive as well as personal data. Its main aim is to secure the data for all the concerned individuals. The data or information which is to be transmitted across a network or to be stored in the same cannot be analyzed by any other third party out of the network. The creator and sender of the message will not be permitted to step back from their intention at a much later stage at the time of transportation or creation of data. This act is known as non-repudiation.
Both the sender and the receiver will be able to confirm the identity of each other before sending out and before receiving the information.

Cryptography And Its Algorithms

The system of cryptography functions with the help of a set of procedures which are also known as cryptographic algorithms or ciphers. These are used for the purpose of both encryption as well as decryption of message for the motive of protecting and securing the process of communication among various devices, computer systems as well as applications. One cipher suite uses up three forms of algorithms. It uses one

algorithm for the process of data encryption. The second algorithm is being used for the purpose of message authentication. And, the third algorithm is used for the process of key exchanging. This entire process remains embedded in the protocols and is also written within the programming language of the software which is used on the operating system together with the systems of computer which are network-based in nature. It includes public generation along with the generation of the private key. The private key is required for both encryption and decryption of information, authentication of message as well as for digital form of signing with the program of key exchange. In simple terms, algorithms can be regarded as the core of cryptography.

CONCLUSION

As you have completed with the teachings of the entire book, now you can easily create a clear image about the processes which are linked with hacking. You will also be able to gain a lot of knowledge about the functioning of Kali Linux. By now, you must have created a clear
perception of all the required tools and components which you need for creating a safe and secure network server for your business and also for personal use. You are the one who is responsible for everything. You alone can secure up an entire system and strengthen up the
infrastructure of security.

With Kali Linux and all its tools, you can easily have complete control over the network security interface related to your business as well as personal network. This book is not solely about Kali Linux as you have also learnt a lot about some of the basic networking components with the security of the same. You can use all the tools from Kali Linux for securing your system. The prime benefit that you can get after using Kali Linux is you can also perform a wide range of tests related to system security. This will ultimately help in wiping out all sorts of susceptibilities and security gaps within your infrastructure of information technology.
What you can do for the security of your system and network depends completely on you. You are the one who can either make it or break it. Ensure that you start using all the steps which you have learnt in this book for securing your system

ABOUT THE AUTHOR

Thomas Kuhn: "The answers you get depend upon the questions you ask."

Harkirat Singh writes books, which, considering where you're reading this, makes perfect sense. He's best known for writing and contributing to various blogs with posts on various topics. A person who always loves to try new field now and then and loves to share his knowledge accured during the journey.

Harkirat is best known for his book on kindel:
Sikh Philosophy & Scriptures

facebook.com/harry.ipsmarty
instagram: @thisharrytales

www.ingramcontent.com/pod-product-compliance
Lightning Source LLC
Chambersburg PA
CBHW051438150726
48000CB00005B/2152